Original title:
Silken Leaves

Copyright © 2025 Creative Arts Management OÜ
All rights reserved.

Author: Lucas Harrington
ISBN HARDBACK: 978-1-80567-059-9
ISBN PAPERBACK: 978-1-80567-139-8

Dance of the Forest in Golden Light

In the forest where whispers giggle,
Trees get tickled and begin to wiggle.
Squirrels in tutus prance with glee,
Giving the branches a chance to see.

Butterflies strut in their fanciest attire,
Making the flowers all burst with desire.
A raccoon winks, wearing shades so cool,
While the rabbits hop high, breaking every rule.

The sunbeams dance, casting shadows that play,
As the critters all join in a grand ballet.
Even the mushrooms are grooving along,
Swaying to nature's outrageous song.

In this woodland rave, there's no need for sleep,
The owls tell jokes that make everyone weep.
With laughter and cheer, the day's nearly done,
But the forest will party till the rise of the sun.

A Harmony Woven Through Green Veins

In the garden, ants plot and scheme,
Wearing tiny hats, a silly dream.
They dance in the sun, the flowers they tease,
While a cat yawns wide, in a cozy breeze.

Butterflies flutter in grand ballet,
Giving bees a fright, running away.
Crickets play tunes on a leaf-made stage,
While frogs hold their breath, in a laughing rage.

Gentle Ripples on Nature's Surface

A fish with a bow tie swims by with flair,
While turtles gossip in their slow, soft lair.
Grasses gossip about clouds so vast,
Chasing their shadows, a moment to last.

A squirrel flips nuts like a grand magician,
Wowing the crowd, it's quite the tradition.
Koalas pretend they're the king of the trees,
Counting the stars while munching on leaves.

Canvas of Dreams Under the Canopy

Pine cones wear crowns, dandelions giggle,
As the wind makes them dance and wiggle.
A troupe of mushrooms, dressed for a show,
In a spotlight of sunlight, they steal the glow.

A raccoon juggles snacks with flair and grace,
While butterflies flutter around his face.
Underneath boughs, where the shadows play,
Laughter erupts, both wild and gay.

Cradled by Nature's Gentle Hands

In the twilight, fireflies flash their bright lights,
Critters team up for late-night delights.
A worm sings a tune that makes us all giggle,
While ants form a line and begin to wiggle.

Mice throw a party in a clover patch,
With cookie crumbs, no one can catch!
Grasshoppers leap into a dance so neat,
While raccoons sneak snacks, their stealthy treat.

Whispers of Gossamer Green

In a garden where shadows play,
A creature in pajamas strayed.
He mistook a leaf for a pillow,
And snoozed there like a sleepy willow.

The ants held a meeting, quite aghast,
'Is this a party or a picnic cast?'
With crumbs of snacks from nearby trees,
They cheered in whispers, 'Oh, yes, please!'

Threads of Nature's Embrace

A spider spun tales with glee,
Of love lost in the fig tree.
Her dreamy webs caught passing flies,
Who swore they heard the laughter rise.

The butterflies, in sparkling attire,
Joined in, their wings like a choir.
They danced with flair, twirled, and spun,
A show of nature, oh what fun!

Breezes Through Velvet Canopies

The wind tickles trees, a playful tease,
Shaking loose acorns, like confetti of peas.
Squirrels hold parties, they laugh out loud,
While birds in the canopy strut like a crowd.

But the clumsy owl fails to woo,
His attempts to dance had the critters askew.
He tried to impress with moves quite absurd,
Yet everyone giggled, oh haven't we heard!

The Dance of Luminous Petals

At dusk, petals began to sway,
With glow worms leading the disarray.
They bumped and jived, oh what a sight,
While frogs croaked critiques about their delight.

A bumblebee buzzed his own tune,
Twisting and twirling, under the moon.
He tripped on a daffodil's hem,
Fell face-first, now part of the gem!

Treading Lightly on Softened Earth

Bouncing on clouds of mushy ground,
Squishy shoes make a comical sound.
With every step, I trip and glide,
Nature's soft carpet, my slippery ride.

Squirrels giggle as I lose my grace,
A froggy leap turns into a race.
The worms are laughing, a jiggly crew,
I'm a clumsy dancer in nature's shoe.

The Dance of Shadows and Light

Sunshine winks through a leafy veil,
Casting shadows like a playful whale.
I do the twist with a twirl and a spin,
Dancing with light like I'm wearing a grin.

The sun plays peek-a-boo, what a sight,
Fleeting figures in a flash of white.
I'm a shadowy jig on the grassy floor,
With each sway, I trip, and then I roar!

Enchantment Amidst the Verdure

In the green expanse, there's magic afoot,
Grass tickles toes, and I hop like a brute.
The flowers chuckle as I skip on by,
A fool in a garden, oh my oh my!

Butterflies tease and flutter around,
While I chase and stumble, feet off the ground.
Each bloom a jester, so loud with cheer,
I'm the laughingstock, but I volunteer!

A Palette of Green and Gold

With colors so bright, I'm an artist at play,
Spilling my paint in a goofy array.
Each brushstroke laughs, and the canvas shakes,
A dappled spectacle that wiggles and quakes.

Golden suns dip low, like they're having a ball,
While I trip on my brush and hilariously fall.
In this colorful chaos, I'm lost in delight,
A fool with a palette, painting the night.

Shimmering Veils of Autumn

A leaf just fell, it made a sound,
Splat! A squirrel spun around.
"What was that?" the critter thought,
As if he'd stumble on a plot.

In colors bright, they wave and sway,
Pretending they can dance all day.
Yet when the wind begins to tease,
They tumble down with funny ease.

Gathered round, the folks all cheer,
For autumn tales, and snacks they near.
But leaves conspire, they're in disguise,
Poking fun right from the skies.

The laughter spreads from tree to tree,
As acorns chuckle, wild and free.
So when you walk and see them fall,
Just smile and join the leaf-y ball!

Tapestry of Soft Light

A patch of gold upon the ground,
A leaf's lost journey, round and round.
On the path, it did a flip,
And nearly caused a fellow's trip.

The sun has dipped, the night is near,
Ghostly leaves dance, bring forth good cheer.
They prance about, a merry crew,
Just waiting for a funny cue.

"What's that?" you ask, a rustling steel,
A leaf that's plotting quite the deal.
A whispered prank, they toss and whirl,
Like toddlers in a playful twirl.

Around the park, the shadows glide,
With moonlit laughter as their guide.
Next time you stroll beneath their light,
Just wink at them, they'll giggle outright!

Caresses of the Twilight Grove

In twilight's glow, a leaf took flight,
Thought it was brave—oh, what a sight!
It twirled and spun through evening air,
Then landed softly, unaware.

Whispers float from trees so grand,
Branches shake, it's all so planned.
The leaves conspire with a chuckle,
"Did you see that? Let's have a snuckle!"

A gust pops up, they sway and squawk,
Drawing laughter in tucked-away nooks.
The forest hums a playful tune,
While critters dance beneath the moon.

So if you hear a rustle or two,
Remember the jokes made just for you.
The twilight grove, alive with jest,
Whisks you away, it's simply the best!

Fluttering Shadows Beneath the Boughs

Under the boughs, a ruckus sounds,
Leaves engage in playful rounds.
A flutter here, a shake over there,
Who knew there'd be such flair in air?

One leaf winks, the other teases,
With giggles shared, it surely pleases.
Darting down like little ninjas,
Their antics spark a whole lot of wind ya.

An acorn shouts, "Hey, what a scene!
These leaf-y pals are full of scheme."
They swirl around with merry hearts,
A leafy show—now, that's some arts!

So join the fun, don't just stand still,
Let the breezy leaf dances thrill.
Beneath the boughs where shadows play,
There's laughter in every leafy sway!

Ethereal Fronds in Morning's Glow

A dance of green upon the breeze,
They tickle noses with such ease.
Whispers of laughter from the trees,
Nature's pranksters, oh, such tease!

Sunlight spills like honeyed juice,
Frogs in tuxedos, quite profuse.
Chirping birds with thoughts of moose,
Nature's giggle - we can't deduce!

Morning fog, a cloak of fun,
Hiding critters on the run.
Curious squirrels, plotting one,
To steal a nut, oh what a pun!

Dewdrops sparkle with a wink,
Puppies chase them, what's the link?
In this world, we dare not blink,
For laughter hides in every clink.

The Weightless Touch of Verdant Realms

Leaves that tickle like a feather,
Float in chaos — oh, such clever!
They play tag with the wind together,
In a game that lasts forever!

Mice wear hats while wiggling by,
Hedged in laughter, oh my, oh my!
Bouncing leaves kiss the sky,
Making jokes – who can deny?

A dandelion shouts, "I'm free!"
Twirly whirls of glee we see.
Bugs join in, with jobs to be,
Working hard with jubilee!

Nature cackles with delight,
As critters plan a froggy flight.
Chasing shadows in the light,
In this dance, all feels just right.

A Symphony of Gentle Colors

Petals chuckle in the sun,
Colors bright as a jolly run.
Laughter echoes, oh, what fun,
Nature's band has just begun!

Butterflies sport silly hats,
Buzzing bees with acrobats.
While grasshoppers engage in spats,
Singing tunes on garden mats!

A rainbow slides down to play,
Winking at clouds, "Come, join the fray!"
Dancing petals glide away,
In a swirl of bright ballet!

Sing away with wooden chimes,
Nature's rhythm, past all crimes.
Each leaf's laughter rises, climbs,
In sweet harmony - oh, what rhymes!

Subtle Hues of the Forest Floor

Mushrooms giggle in a line,
Whispering secrets, oh divine!
A carpet of laughter they define,
As sunlight breaks through, looking fine.

Crickets serenade the night,
With clumsy steps, they take flight.
Bouncing berries, such a sight,
Dancing in the soft moonlight!

Froggies croak their funny song,
In the forest, they belong.
Roots wrap around, strong yet wrong,
Playful jests are never long!

Napping leaves hear tales so grand,
Chuckling softly, hand in hand.
For in this land, they all stand,
With rhythms steady, life is planned.

Cargo of the Verdant Refuge

In a garden of loot, treasures abound,
Mischief unfolds, where giggles are found.
A squirrel in a hat, claiming a stash,
Dancing with acorns, oh what a splash!

Beneath the bright sun, the daisies compete,
They wiggle their petals, a comical feat.
The broccoli waves, its arms in the air,
"Eat me if you dare!" it shouts with a flair.

Shades of Tranquil Enchantment.

In the woods where shadows play peek-a-boo,
Mushrooms wear hats like a fancy brew.
A moth tells the tale of its drunken brawl,
"I won't pick a side, I just love them all!"

The tree branches sway like they're having a dance,
In this goofy ballet, not a leaf takes a chance.
A twig gives a speech, but it's lost in the breeze,
"I promise it's great!" then falls with such ease.

Whispers of the Wistful Canopy

Bubbles of laughter float high in the air,
As the pine trees gossip, without a care.
A frog on a lily, wearing a tie,
Sings of romance, oh me, oh my!

The bees throw a party, with nectar so sweet,
While ants do the conga, oh what a treat!
The flowers turn pink, from laughter so loud,
In this joyous jungle, they're all feeling proud.

Tapestry of Gentle Green

On a hill made of marshmallows, fluffy and bright,
Llamas in pajamas, what a silly sight!
They skip and they hop, with laughs all around,
In this whimsical world, where joy can be found.

The butterflies argue, 'Who's prettiest here?'
While frogs play the judge, grinning from ear to ear.
A snail rolls its eyes, tired of the game,
And shouts, "I am slow, but I'll win just the same!"

A Canvas of Whispering Shades

In the garden, colors bloom,
Tickling noses, dispelling gloom.
Dancing petals, clever and bright,
A parade of shades, quite the sight.

Bees in bow ties, buzzing with flair,
Complaining about flowers in their hair.
Butterflies wearing socks, it's a show,
Nature's own circus, ticket prices low.

Sunlight splatters like thrown paint,
Every leaf a comical saint.
With giggles in the air, who could resist?
Not even the toad, who's plotting a twist!

In this wild art, joy steals the scene,
Nature's canvas, bright and green.
So grab your brush, come laugh, come play,
In a world where whimsy leads the way.

Veils of Enchantment in the Garden

A dress of vines, swaying with grace,
Giggling flowers in a lovely embrace.
Lizards wear crowns made of petal and dew,
While rabbits play hopscotch, it's nothing new.

The gnomes stand guard in their pointed hats,
While squirrels exchange gossip with the chitchat of bats.

With every rustle, secrets they weave,
As the sun gives a wink, just try not to leave!

The wind throws confetti from trees overhead,
Whispering jokes that tickle the bread.
A garden fête where the blooms gossip right,
And the daisies debate the best dance at night.

So join in the fun, pull up a chair,
Where flowers tell stories without a care.
Every petal's a punchline waiting to share,
In this magical patch, laughter fills the air.

The Weight of Whispering Flora

The stems are strong, but oh, so light,
Daisies debating the best flight.
Flowers flex in a botanical gym,
Making leaves giggle with every whim.

In the shade, a lazy frog gripes,
"Why do the flowers wear so many stripes?"
While butterflies tease with a wink and a flutter,
As daisies roll over in grateful mutter.

The daisies have dreams of wild, wild heights,
Doing cartwheels and somersault flights.
But who will catch them if they fall,
With rhymes from the trees as their curtain call?

Laughter erupts at the gnarled old tree,
"Let's form a band, just you and me!"
"Who needs the wind? We'll croon on our own!"
In this botanical show, whimsy has grown.

Soft Echoes of Nature's Caress

Whispers of green dance on the breeze,
Laughter echoes between the trees.
Each soft rustle a giggle, it seems,
As petals spill secrets, chasing their dreams.

A wandering snail in a polka dot shell,
Tells tales of his travels, oh, wouldn't you dwell?
While dandelions chuckle, playing hide-and-seek,
In a game where the fun hides, never too bleak.

Nectar-fed sprites with sugary grins,
Spread laughter like sunbeams from leaf-laden bins.
The ladybugs waltz, what a curious sight,
As the weeds try to steal the show every night.

Under the moon, the petals all sway,
Sending giggles through the night and the day.
Let's join the ruckus, get swept up in cheer,
In the grand garden circus, so lively, so near!

Dappled Light Upon the Forest Floor

In the woods, where sunlight plays,
Little critters have wild ways.
Squirrels chase their own tails true,
While mushrooms wear hats of dew.

The shadows stretch and twist around,
A raccoon spies a nut he found.
He fumbles with his little paws,
Then trips and flops—what a round of applause!

A bird attempts to sing a tune,
But ends up sounding like a loon.
The trees all giggle, leaves aflutter,
While ants hold tight to crumbs of butter.

So stroll with glee across the glade,
And laugh at nature's silly parade.
For in this vibrant chuckle fest,
The forest shows us life at its best.

The Poetry of Rustling Foliage

Amidst the leaves, a whisper flows,
A squirrel's chatter, I suppose.
He thinks he's Shakespeare—oh how grand!
But all he has is acorns on hand!

The trees recite with rustling flair,
Their branches waving—do they care?
A gust of wind, a dramatic pause,
As if they're critiquing their own cause.

The bushes chuckle at a tumbleweed,
Who rolls by fast, a hapless steed.
All nature laughs; it's quite the scene,
In this green theater, so serene.

Let's join the fun, let laughter bloom,
As foliage dances, dispelling gloom.
For understudies in this grand plot,
We find our joy in every jot.

Caressing the Earth: A Verdant Saga

In the meadow, grass gets frisky,
Inviting bugs for a dance quite risky.
A butterfly slips, a comical slide,
While daisies giggle, unashamed wide.

The earthworms squirm with glee underground,
Throwing parties, oh, what a sound!
With dirt cake served under the stars,
And fireflies counting their little cars.

A fox watches, with a grin so sly,
He knows he's the king, oh my oh my!
As blossoms blush in hues so bright,
He struts around, a true delight.

Nature's comedy, oh such a joy,
Where every seed is a giggling toy.
So take your stroll and join the cheer,
For in this green world, laughter's near.

Shadows Danced by the Wind

Under branches, shadows play,
Where the breeze has something to say.
A leaf flutters, giving a wink,
As if it knows what we all think.

The shadow of a pouncing cat,
Hides near a log, oh imagine that!
But with a tumble, he trips and yelps,
The forest bursts with giggles and kelps.

A dandelion wishes on a whim,
To be a star, but its chances look dim.
Yet, it smiles as the wind twists it free,
Saying, "I'm perfect, just let me be!"

So dance your way through the leafy lines,
And join the fun where humor shines.
In shadows or sun, let laughter be,
The tune of nature, wild and free.

Where the Earth Meets the Sky

The clouds wore hats and danced around,
While birds chirped jokes, a laugh profound.
But then a squirrel slipped on a cloud,
And fell down laughing, all proud and loud.

The sun peeked down, a curious grin,
While shadows of trees played hide and spin.
A butterfly tripped, fell on its face,
And laughed with the flowers in a sunny embrace.

The grass sang songs of the silly breeze,
Tickling the toes of the passing bees.
While a cheeky worm told puns so bold,
Every story it spun turned to gold.

In this patch of giggles and sunny cheer,
Nature tickles, bringing joy near.
Where sky meets ground, life sways and plays,
And laughter echoes through all the days.

Musings of the Wind-Kissed Branches

Branches whisper, 'What do you see?'
The wind replies, 'Your dance looks free!'
A twig jokes, 'I'm a flying stick!'
But really, it just wants a better trick.

Leaves are giggling, swaying in tune,
As squirrels plot under the watchful moon.
One leaf said, 'I'll float to the ground!'
But forgot it was stuck—how silly it found!

A feather joined in with a fluttery grace,
Declaring, 'I'm here for a breezy race!'
But landed flat on a sleepy flower,
And there it snoozed for a half an hour.

Amidst this chaos, a chatty twig,
Called out, 'Hey there! Let's all dance big!'
With chuckles and chortles, they twirled with glee,
In the wind's warm embrace, they laughed wild and free.

The Heartbeat of the Verdant Glade

In the glade where giggles meet,
Frogs wear crowns, and mushrooms greet.
A toad jumped as if on a spring,
And landed right in a dandelion ring.

Crickets chirp offbeat tunes,
Each chord scattering, like silly balloons.
A ladybug lands, but looks quite shy,
Saying, 'I'm just here to wave goodbye!'

The bushes gossip about bumblebees,
Whispering sweet nothings on a cool breeze.
A rabbit slips, does a comical fall,
And the chortling flowers witness it all.

In this heartbeat of green, laughter grows,
With each little blunder, a tale reflows.
Nature's humor, a joyful parade,
Where hilarity thrives, and worries fade.

Echoes of Serenity Amongst the Crowns

Under leafy crowns, a secret club,
Where acorns joke and shy buds rub.
A parrot squawks, 'I'm the king of fun!'
While a turtle spins tales—but just one.

The flowers gossip, 'What a sight!'
As bees flirt under the soft moonlight.
One leaf said, 'I'll roll down the lane!'
But tripped on a root, feeling quite lame.

The trees chuckle as branches sway,
While a gentle breeze adds to the play.
'Wanna race?' said one branch with flair,
But got tangled up, caught in mid-air.

Laughter dances through the green and gold,
Every giggle a story waiting to be told.
In the heart of the woods, joy overflows,
With echoes of fun in all that it shows.

A Journey Through Verdant Vistas

In a world of green delights,
Frogs in hats dance with might.
Squirrels juggling nuts, oh dear,
Chasing shadows, full of cheer.

Underneath the leafy shade,
A lazy cat has fully laid.
Chasing dreams of feathered prey,
With a yawn, it slips away.

Bouncing bugs, a wacky show,
Tickle grass, and watch it grow!
In this garden, oddity reigns,
Laughter echoes through the lanes.

Prancing about, a fox in socks,
He quips with glee, and jokes with flocks.
In this vernal, funny plight,
Every moment feels just right.

Harmony in the Canopy's Embrace

Under branches full of glee,
A parrot sings off-key.
Monkeys share a laughing fit,
While a turtle claims he's it!

Breezes whisper funny tales,
Of clumsy cats and fishy scales.
Swaying branches, a goofy dance,
Even the bugs join in the prance.

An owl hoots a cheerful tune,
Dancing 'neath a glowing moon.
Each rustle brings a chuckle near,
Nature's jesters cast their cheer.

Leafy pals in jestful plays,
Sunbeams warm the light-filled rays.
Every giggle fills the air,
A joyous song beyond compare.

A Breath of Springtime's Tender Touch

In the spring, where giggles bloom,
Bunnies wiggle, chase, and zoom.
Frogs in bow ties hop around,
Making music, silly sound.

An old snail slips in a race,
With a smile upon its face.
Butterflies, all dressed to thrill,
Flit around, they laugh and chill.

Pigeons strut like fashion kings,
While a hedgehog tunes its strings.
The grass tickles, they all roll,
Joy abounds, that's the goal.

Dewdrops glisten, playful sight,
Morning sun, pure delight.
A chirpy tune from trees above,
Nature's giggle, filled with love.

Lyrical Breezes Through the Glades

Winds whisper secrets of delight,
As trees sway left and right.
A dancing deer tries to sing,
But ends up tripping on a string!

Chipmunks dressed in vibrant stripes,
Host a party full of gripes.
Each nut tossed in great debate,
Turns into a wobbly fate!

In the glade, a grand parade,
Of critters singing, unafraid.
Joyful chirps and clapping paws,
Nature's jam without a pause.

With laughter echoing through the trees,
Squirrels spin in merry freezes.
Each playful twirl, a silly tease,
Music floats upon the breeze.

Tender Resilience in the Woodland

In the woods where squirrels play,
Turtles dance, hip hip hooray!
Mushrooms giggle in the shade,
Nature's charm will never fade.

Lively critters bust a move,
In the breeze, they find their groove.
Bees are buzzing, singing loud,
Even trees are feeling proud.

Each leaf winks with healthy glee,
"Watch me twist!" says one small tree.
Rabbits hop in fancy pants,
Who knew woods could make you dance?

So if you're feeling rather blue,
Join the show, there's fun for two.
Nature's laughter light as air,
Leaves and critters, secret fair!

Where the Wild Unfurls in Silence

In a hush, the wild things plot,
Squirrels steal a fiendish nut.
Hedgehogs wear their spiky hats,
And do a jig, much like acrobats.

Worms complain of dampened days,
While snails take their snazzy lays.
"Not so fast!" a frog declares,
As wildflowers put on airs.

The grasses wag, they shake and sway,
Chasing clouds, they joke and play.
Nature's laughter fills the space,
In this quiet, giggly place.

So welcome to this silly scene,
Where sounds of joy stay evergreen.
The wild unfurls, so lush and bright,
With messy smiles, it feels just right!

Breathings of a Dreamy Landscape

In a land of sleepy dreams,
Waking flowers plot their schemes.
Softly giggles brush the grass,
While dandelions wave en masse.

Clouds like sheep drift overhead,
As crickets sing their tunes in bed.
Moonbeams stretch with graceful flair,
Making shadows dance with care.

Frogs wear crowns of rusty leaves,
Whisper secrets, share their thieves.
A bumblebee tumbles, so uncharmed,
In this dreamland, all's disarmed.

So let's embrace this whimsical plot,
Where every creature laughs a lot.
Breathings of the landscape's cheer,
A bedtime story bright and clear!

The Melody of Branches Against Time

Branches sway with giggles fine,
Whistling tunes like aged wine.
The playful breeze, a joker sly,
Tells the trees, "Oh, you can fly!"

Bark wears wrinkles like a grin,
Every year's a cheeky spin.
Owls hoot jokes that make no sense,
While mice chuckle in their fence.

"Hey! I saw that leaf fall down!"
Squeaks a squirrel in a crown.
With a flip, it hops back up,
Nature's laughter fills the cup.

Steady branches hold the tune,
Onward, we'll sway 'neath the moon.
The melody, a timeless rhyme,
Dances lightly, laughing time!

Gentle Murmurs in the Thicket

In the morning light, squirrels dance,
Chasing shadows, a silly romance.
Leaves whisper secrets, oh what a tease,
A chatty breeze tickles the trees.

The careless chipmunk with snacks so grand,
Tripped on a twig, oh wasn't it planned?
He stumbled and tumbled with wide-eyed glee,
Nature's circus, come laugh with me!

A fox in a bow tie, quite the sight,
Debating a rabbit in broad daylight.
"Who wore it better?" they muse with a grin,
Nature's runway—let the show begin!

The flowers giggle, their petals aflutter,
"Why do bees buzz? Just can't keep quiet!"
The thicket chuckles, sends ripples of fun,
Murmurs of mischief until day is done.

Silhouettes of Delicate Dreams

Beneath the starlight, crickets conspire,
In the moon's glow, their jokes never tire.
A sleepy owl hoots, then cracks a joke,
"Ever tried laughing while perched on a oak?"

The hedgehog twirls, a dance so absurd,
While a badger just stares, not saying a word.
"Do you think I could join? Just look at my spines!"
But he's not one for dancing, despite his designs.

A rabbit with glasses reads all the news,
"Did you hear about that new carrot cruise?"
The forest bursts out in whimsical cheer,
As shadows of dreams bring the silly near.

Flickering fireflies glow in delight,
As they giggle and flare, igniting the night.
Whispering stories like young schoolmates,
While the moon rolls her eyes at their silly debates.

Opalescent Layers of Dawn

Morning arrives with a wink and a nod,
A rooster yells, "You've all been a fraud!"
The sun peeks out with a cheeky grin,
"Did you sleep well? Let the fun begin!"

The dew drops glisten like jewels on the ground,
A playful puppy leaps, spinning around.
"Watch me! I'm a rocket!" he barks with glee,
As breakfast crumbs fly—all over the tree!

A bunch of birds gather, gossip and chatter,
"What's this about worms? I thought they were fatter!"
And just then a worm pops up for a peek,
"Just a few more squats, then I'll be sleek!"

As layers of morning melt into day,
Nature's laughter leads us all on our way.
With jokes in the air and smiles that bloom,
The dawn wraps us up in its bright, funny room.

Hushed Symphony of the Woods

In the forest's heart, a nonsense parade,
Creatures assemble, no plans to evade.
The bear wears a hat, is that quite a trick?
While the raccoon's on stage telling jokes really quick.

An orchestra starts with the chirps and the croaks,
With frogs on the bass and owls just as folks.
"Let's do a duet!" croaks a cheeky young toad,
But his rhythm's too off—it's a wobbly road.

Branches sway gently, like a dance on the floor,
A couple of squirrels just can't take it anymore.
"Did you hear the one about the tree and the bee?"
Then bursts into laughter, as happy as can be.

As twilight descends, the symphony plays,
With the wind as the maestro, leading the way.
In the hush of the woods, where giggles convene,
Nature's humor unites, sparkling and keen.

Beneath the Whisper of Ancients

Under the shade, wise ones convene,
Chattering squirrels join in the scene.
A feathered bard drops a joke so sly,
While pondering clouds that wander by.

The old oak chuckles with creaky delight,
As ants march home with crumbs all night.
Who knew the branches held such cheer?
In the forest's heart, joy's crystal clear!

Mice in twirls dance on blades of green,
In this merry grove, not a frown to be seen.
The breeze tickles jokes from leaf to leaf,
Turning frowns to laughter, not just belief.

So hear the elders share their thoughts,
Life's too grand to tie in knots.
With giggles and wiggles, nature's embrace,
Under sprawling limbs, we find our place.

A Serenade Composed in the Greenery

A frog in a tux croaks classical tunes,
While bumblebees buzz like tiny balloons.
Grass blades sway to the music's beat,
Bringing rhythm to the summer's heat.

The daisies dance, with petals so bright,
Cracking jokes with a guy in flight.
A robin's wink, quick as a flash,
Makes the daisies giggle and dash!

All critters join, from squirrel to bee,
In a comical show, they frolic with glee.
The willow bends low with a bow so grand,
As laughter erupts across the land.

Nature's concert brings smiles galore,
In this charming world, we always want more.
In shades of green, our joy ignites,
With every rustle, our spirits take flight.

The Stillness of a Solitary Leaf

Hanging alone, a leaf thinks it bold,
Dodging the wind with tales often told.
It dreams of a dance, perhaps a great leap,
While giggling squirrels gossip and peep.

The world below, in frantic spins,
As critters juggle their tiny wins.
But the leaf holds tight, with a wink and a grin,
Waiting for laughter to swirl from within.

Ah! What a show, down on the ground,
A raccoon dramatically twirling around.
The leaf can't help but sway with delight,
Wishing for legs, but it's stuck with flight.

Stillness can be quite a tricky affair,
With chuckles and chuckles floating in air.
So here's to the leaf, with its comical stance,
A silent observer, of nature's wild dance.

Nature's Embrace of Vitality and Grace

In the meadow, a party's in swing,
Butterflies waltz while crickets all sing.
A dragonfly juggles, quite out of sight,
A banner of laughter, oh what a sight!

The daisies beam bright, in a floral parade,
Tickling the toes of a frog quite displayed.
Each petal and stem, with humor they blend,
In this playful dance that will never end.

As the sun dips low, the fun escalates,
A snail on a scooter, oh, how it fascinates!
The wind whispers secrets to trees in their prime,
Sharing giggles with nature, just passing the time.

So let's toast to the wild, where the giggles are grand,
To the joyous creatures that roam upon land.
In nature's embrace, we find our own pace,
In the dance of the wild, we've all found our place.

Twilit Fabrics of Earth

Underneath the twilight skies,
Fabrics dance like fireflies.
Whispers tickle grassy blades,
While squirrels wear their leafy shades.

Twirling in a mimic's show,
The bushes giggle, 'Look at Joe!'
He trips and tumbles, laughs abound,
As petals flutter all around.

With colors bright, a comical sight,
The branches swing with pure delight.
As if the forest loves to tease,
And mess around with the gentle breeze.

Nature's pranks, oh what a treat,
Each leaf and twig, in playful beat.
Beneath the moon's soft, silvery gleam,
The earth wears joy, a vibrant dream.

Glimmers Among the Foliage

Glimmers hide where shadows creep,
The leaves are plotting, not a peep.
Frogs in hats play checkers there,
While mice on stilts pretend to care.

Sunbeams giggle through the trees,
As if they're sharing silly teas.
Petal pirates sail the air,
With dandelion ships, beware!

Squirrels dressed in polka dots,
Steal acorns from the elder's pots.
Laughter rings without a lock,
In every crevice, every rock.

What mischief hides in leafy folds?
A tale of whimsy, life unfolds.
Glimmers twinkle, secrets shared,
In the woodland, no one's scared.

Ethereal Touch of the Sylvan Realm

Moonlit sprites on leaves do prance,
Under a starry, dreamy dance.
Owls in glasses read their books,
While raccoons give the funniest looks.

Giggles echo through the night,
As fireflies join the wiggle fight.
Branches sway to the playful beat,
While hedgehogs polish their tiny feet.

With every rustle, antics play,
Nature's comedy—hip hip hooray!
The forest floor a stage so grand,
Where chuckles bloom like grains of sand.

In this place where dreams collide,
The spirit of fun cannot hide.
Each creature shares a merry song,
In the realm where laughter belongs.

Filaments of Tender Transition

In the breeze, they twist and turn,
Old leaves giggle, new ones learn.
Chasing shadows, tickling air,
A joyful game, no one can spare.

Gossamer threads weave tales anew,
While crickets hum a comical tune.
The world spins round in every shade,
As silly puppets sway and parade.

With every flutter, jokes unfold,
Colanders for crowns, tales bold.
In the forest, life takes flight,
A carnival of pure delight.

Tender moments, laughter bright,
A tapestry of pure delight.
In the rustle of a fading leaf,
Is hidden joy, beyond belief.

Veils of Nature's Embrace

In the garden, the plants have a chat,
One asks, "Where's that pesky cat?"
They giggle as twigs tangle and twist,
Who knew nature had a sense of humor, not a mist?

The flowers dance in a vibrant parade,
Swaying to a tune that never will fade,
But bees buzz in, with a comical sting,
"Hey, I was dancing!" the daisies all sing!

The breeze tickles leaves, oh what a sight,
Whispers of secrets, a feathered delight,
Frogs on their lily pads hold a debate,
"Who's the best croaker?" Oh, don't make me wait!

So revel in nature's playful display,
Where laughter and joy frolic and play,
In the embrace of the world, pure and bright,
Let's join the chuckles till the fall of night.

Fluttering Dreams in the Breeze

Butterflies argue, 'Who's the prettiest here?'
"It's me!" screams a monarch, as others cheer,
But a bumblebee hums, "What's all the fuss?"
"I make the honey, let's make a big fuss!"

The wind blows softly, a tickle on skin,
"Hey, stop that!" the daisies yell with a grin,
They lean to the right, swaying with glee,
Life's a fun game, as free as can be!

Clouds roll by like a fluffy parade,
Each shape resembles a plan that we made,
A dragon, a ship, now what's that, a cow?
Oh! More like a tuber! Let's rename it now!

In this whimsical world, joy captures hearts,
Where laughter and giggles are classic arts,
So flutter along on this playful breeze,
In nature's soft lap, let's find our ease.

Echoes Beneath the Shaded Boughs

Under the trees, a raccoon holds court,
His royal decree? "Keep quiet!" he sort,
But the squirrels keep chattering, causing a ruck,
"Shhh, we're hiding! We're not out of luck!"

Mice bring the popcorn for a movie night show,
As owls drop in with eyes all aglow,
"Is this seat taken?" they ask with a hoot,
"Only if you bring snacks!" was the firm loot.

The shadows invite all creatures in line,
To join in the fun under branches that twine,
Laughter is echoed in the ring of the leaves,
As critters conspire, oh, what a reprieve!

So gather, my friends, let stories unfold,
Under the shelter so cozy and bold,
In echoes of nature, humor gets free,
Where joy abounds in each whispering tree.

A Soft Caress in the Meadow

In soft meadows, the daisies play games,
Each one boasts loudly, calling out names,
"Look at me sunny," a bright one shouts proud,
While a tiny weed giggles, "I'm really a cloud!"

The grass tickles toes, "Oh, what a surprise!"
Nature made mischief, oh how it can rise,
A butterfly thinks it's a ballerina,
"Just one more twirl, I'm a diva, see ya!"

Bumblebees buzz with a comedic song,
"Dance along punks, you're all doing it wrong!"
They dizzy the daisies with a swirling band,
In this happy meadow, life's perfectly planned!

So frolic and tumble, let giggles take flight,
Join the procession of pure sheer delight,
In the softness of the world, find laughter anew,
In a playful embrace, where joy's the best view!

Celestial Tints in Nature's Thread

In the park, colors whirled,
Little squirrels with tails unfurled.
They dance in joy, a comedic spree,
While birds chirp tunes of pure jubilee.

Pinks and blues in wild delight,
A rainbow's joke, oh what a sight!
Who knew grass could strut and boast?
While daisies chuckle, they're the host!

Sunbeams wink, tickling trees,
Nature's laughter floats on the breeze.
The plants gossip, oh what a fuss,
With whispers of laughter, who's next to discuss?

So come, my friend, join this jest,
In hues of nature, we're truly blessed.
Life's a canvas, let's make it bright,
With humor woven in every light!

Unfolding Chapters in the Wild

Once, a leaf wore a pirate hat,
Claiming treasures from bushes and mat.
Butterflies giggled at the bold flair,
While flowers swayed with mischievous air.

The trees tell tales of playful pranks,
Sticks telling secrets in playful ranks.
With rustles and whoops, a woodland tease,
As mushrooms erupt, dancing with ease.

An owl grinned, wearing glasses askew,
While crickets chimed in, with a giggle or two.
The flora writes stories where laughter spills,
In nature's pages, mirth gently thrills.

So come flip a page, let's laugh and roam,
In chapters of green, we can call home.
With whimsy and chuckles, let the feast commence,
In the wild's merry tales, life is immense!

The Gentle Ebb of Season's Change

As autumn flutters, leaves take flight,
A tumble and twist, a comical sight.
Trees shed their jackets, giggling profusely,
While the wind kicks up dancing profusely.

Winter arrives, snowflakes on parade,
They tickle the noses, the fun never fades.
Squirrels in puffs, hopping with cheer,
While frostbitten flowers bring laughter near.

Spring springs forth with plants in a race,
Who blooms the fastest, a lively chase!
Tulips nudge daffodils, tickling pink,
As blossoms burst laughter with a wink.

Summer then yawns, sun high and bright,
Cicadas strum tunes in warm delight.
With laughter flowing, seasons embrace,
In nature's humor, we find our place!

Emerald Dreams in a Sunlit Glade

In a glade of green, where laughter thrives,
Tiny frogs croak their jolly jives.
The daisies laugh, with petals aglow,
Tickling the ferns, in a radiant show.

A rabbit hops, with style, so grand,
Wearing a top hat, he takes a stand.
He jests with the breeze, a easygoing charm,
While butterflies giggle, spreading warm.

The sun giggles, casting jade light,
Making shadows dance, a whimsical sight.
In this dreamy glade where fun intertwines,
Even the bumblebees share in the signs.

So join this revel, in emerald hues,
Where nature's laughter ignites our views.
In the glade of dreams, let's frolic and play,
With smiles woven in the bright ballet!

The Art of the Quiet Grove

In the grove where critters creep,
A squirrel danced while I took a leap.
With twigs and leaves upon my head,
I struck a pose; the trees just said.

A whisper here, a giggle there,
The owls wink, like they just don't care.
With every rustle, laughter grows,
While I trip over my own toes.

The frogs croak jokes beneath the moon,
While fireflies blink a silly tune.
I tried to prance with elegance,
But stumbled right into the fence.

Yet every bruise just adds to charm,
As woodland sprites call me a harm.
In this grove, I'm a jester bold,
With stories that are never told!

Lush Echoes of the Wooded Realm

In leafy halls where shadows play,
A raccoon steals my picnic tray.
The trees start laughing in the breeze,
As squirrels chatter, doing as they please.

A deer pranced by, in quite a rush,
Thought I was lunch; oh what a crush!
But rather than get stuck in fear,
I clutched my sandwich and gave a cheer!

Mushrooms giggle as I trip and fall,
The brambles poke; I hear their call.
Around my ankle, vines do weave,
I wave goodbye; I mustn't grieve!

These woods are filled with snickers and snorts,
With jesters clad in fuzzy shorts.
Though clumsy I roam, I'm never alone,
In this realm, all laughter's grown!

The Serenade of Fragrant Petals

In gardens bright with blooms so bold,
I twirl and spin, or so I'm told.
Yet while I dance, a bee flies near,
With my buttery moves, it's clear I'm dear!

Petals trip me in a fragrant whirl,
As butterflies laugh, they start to twirl.
With every whiff, I lose my grace,
Then land right in a flower's embrace!

I tried to sing, but sounded weird,
The roses blushed; I think they cheered.
But daisies whispered among themselves,
"Oh look, there goes that fool of elves!"

Yet laughter fills this floral hall,
Where even clumsy prancers do enthrall.
In scents of sweetness, I find my tune,
Amidst the petaled, giggling tune!

Hushed Murmurs in Autumn's Chill

In fields of gold where whispers blend,
The wind tickles, making me bend.
I'm leaping over piles of crunch,
Then get stuck in a leaf-filled hunch!

A crow caws loudly, cracking a jest,
While I pretend I'm on a quest.
With acorns tumbling down like rain,
I dodge and weave—oh what a pain!

A chilly breeze starts blowing fast,
I act like I'm a leaf, surpassed.
But as I float, I hit a tree,
What fun this fall is, can't you see?

While winter waits with frosty breath,
I'll chase the leaves until my death.
But for now, I laugh and twirl with glee,
In autumn's arms, just wild and free!

Carpet of Life Underfoot

In the garden of toe-socks, they gleefully sprout,
Dancing in sunlight, with laughter they shout.
Each step's a surprise, like a tickle and tease,
Who knew life's a plaything beneath our bare knees?

They whisper of secrets we tread on with flair,
Swirling around as we float in the air.
Are they soft little cushions or ticklish spies?
They grin as we stumble, they giggle our sighs.

We trip over giggles, we slip on a grin,
Waltzing with wonder, the game's about to begin.
With each little misstep, life's absurdity grows,
They're not just our flooring, they're the stars of the show!

So let's jump on this carpet, let's frolic and spin,
Each patch is a story, where silliness wins.
From rain to bright sunshine, it's quite the delight,
Together we shimmy, oh what a fun sight!

Forest Dreams in Twilight Hues

In the woods where shadows play tricks on the eyes,
The squirrels are plotters with acorn-filled ties.
They claim they're just gathering for winter's grand feast,

But I swear that they're scheming, to have a wild yeast!

Trees stretch and yawn as the daylight takes flight,
They shake off the slumber, ready to bite.
With branches like arms, they reach out for a hug,
'Cause who needs a friend when you're snug as a bug?

A fox runs by, wearing nuggety shoes,
Trying to boast of his fanciest moves.
With each little leap, he lands in a heap,
Nature's hilarious show, where we all get to peep!

At dusk, when the laughter and chatter entwine,
The forest spills secrets, like aged, fruity wine.
So dance with the shadows, and chuckle with glee,
In twilight's embrace, we're forever carefree!

Green Hues of Rejuvenation and Peace

Beneath the thick ferns where the gnomes tend their farms,
They stir up the soil with peculiar charms.
'Tis true, they've got dreams of a tiny green car,
But all they can drive is the slow-growing tar!

The sprouts are in fashion, with leaves that can swing,
They twirl in the breeze, like a wiggly spring.
With petals that giggle, they play peek-a-boo,
'Catch me if you can!' says the bright velvet dew!

Moss nods in agreement, so plush and so bold,
Unfurling in laughter, refusing to scold.
A dance of small creatures, in jackets of green,
They twinkle and flicker, a comical scene!

So wander through patches where giggles take flight,
With twinkling leaves whispering joy through the night.
The hues of renewal, a charming delight,
Nature's own jesters, spreading laughter so bright!

Where Nature's Heart Beats Softly

In the glen where the critters have round-table talks,
They argue and ponder, while hopping like socks.
Each flower a diplomat, voting for cheer,
While bees buzz around, their policies clear!

The brook's bubbling laughter, a tickling sound,
While turtles debate how to walk in a round.
With snails as the judges, their pace is so slow,
Who knew this was where humor would grow?

Butterflies glide in their fluttery suits,
While ants march in lines to deliver all fruits.
They gossip and giggle, with raucous delight,
Shouting, "Look at the clouds, aren't they quite a sight?"

So come join this party, beneath boughs so wide,
Where laughter's contagious and joy's set to ride.
For nature's own heart beats with whimsical glee,
In this merriment dance, where all spirits run free!

Filigree of Branches Against the Sky

Branches twist and turn, so spry,
Birds misjudge their landing, oh my!
With each gust they do a dance,
And squirrels are caught in a trance.

A strand of leaves with a wink,
Caught in mid-air, take a drink.
Nature's humor, a leafy tease,
Laughter echoes on the breeze.

Breezy antics sway and shake,
Mimicking all the silly flake.
Each branch bowing with delight,
While shadows play in morning light.

With each gust, a giggle blooms,
As nature booms in funny rooms.
A frolicsome jig on display,
In the branches, come what may.

The Graceful Sway of Healing Nature

Nature stretches, a yoga pose,
Flexing branches, it surely knows.
Healing vibes on every swing,
Leaves giggle as they sprout and cling.

Dandelions laugh with glee,
Casting wishes for you and me.
Bumblebees buzz in a row,
Playing tag, away they go!

Grass tickles toes, a soft delight,
As clouds drift slowly, out of sight.
Nature's laughter, light and free,
Reminds us all to just be silly.

In every shade, a chuckle hides,
As sunlight dances and glides.
The healing shade, it softly sways,
To the rhythm of playful rays.

A Symphony in Green Tones

Rustling leaves compose a tune,
In the morning, beneath the moon.
Each flutter adds to nature's song,
In a melody where we belong.

Chirping crickets drop a beat,
While frogs join in, oh so sweet.
With laughter layered through the air,
Everything joins in, none a care.

Branches sway, a smooth ballet,
As direct from nature's cabaret.
All flora bops to the delight,
Of a bright, unusual night.

A symphony of gusts and giggles,
In the dance of nature, there are wiggles.
In this orchestra, join the fun,
As green tones bloom and laughter run.

Petals Whispering Secrets to the Stars

Under a moon that plays peek-a-boo,
Petals gossip, just me and you.
Secrets shared on a cool night air,
With twinkling stars as their affair.

The daisies giggle, oh so coy,
While roses flirt with all their joy.
In every whisper, a chuckle gleams,
As nature weaves its playful dreams.

Jokesters fluttering without a care,
Spreading chuckles through the warm air.
Petals murmur, soft and light,
Filing stories till the night.

As stars wink down with a sly grin,
Nature's ensemble welcomes in.
Secrets shared beneath the sky,
In every rustle, a happy sigh.

www.ingramcontent.com/pod-product-compliance
Lightning Source LLC
Chambersburg PA
CBHW072139200426
43209CB00051B/137